JAPANDI STYLE

When Japanese and Scandinavian Designs Blend

AGATA & PIERRE TOROMANOFF

JAPANDI STYLE

When Japanese and Scandinavian Designs Blend

MERRELL
LONDON • NEW YORK

CONTENTS

INTRODUCTION

Japandi style, the newest design trend of the 21st century, is rooted in the striking similarities – both obvious and paradoxical – between the aspirations of Nordic design and the traditions of Japanese craftsmanship. Despite the geographic distance, which prevented the development of cultural interactions until the beginning of the 20th century, and despite the very different lifestyles and ways of using space, the fascinating convergence of the aesthetics and values that guide the designers in both regions is clear. The care taken with the finish of objects and the attention to detail, the purity of the simple and timeless shapes, often inspired by nature, and the use of soft, muted colors are all common principles that underline the affinity between the two design schools. One could also mention the predilection for organic materials and the imperative of sustainability that drives both Scandinavian designers and their Japanese counterparts.

While some design studios bring together designers from Scandinavia and Japan in an attempt to create a style that draws on the best of each school, Japandi style is more about initiating a dialogue in which each party is enriched by the experience of the other, a search for complementarity and compatibility, in which the understanding and assimilation of mutual merits is essential. This book is written in the same spirit.

The first part examines the converging principles that have contributed to the emergence of Japandi style, such as simplicity and functionality, muted colors, the importance of organic materials, and the thoughtful minimalism of shapes, before going on to present some of the most emblematic works of Japandi design and the studios behind them. In the third chapter, we will see how to decorate and furnish rooms – the entrance, living room, dining room, bedroom, children's room, kitchen, bathroom, home office, and terrace – in Japandi style.

Above: Rooms in a home should be designed to provide rest for the body and mind.

Page 2: Brightness, comfort, and simple shapes – whether geometric or organic – are at the heart of Japandi style.

Page 4: Soft colors and natural materials transform this bedroom designed by the Swedish brand Ellos into a simple and warm haven of peace.

CHAPTER 1

What makes Nordic and Japanese design traditions so similar?

SIMPLICITY AND FUNCTIONALITY

When we consider the similarities between Japanese and Scandinavian design, simplicity and functionality spontaneously come to mind. These qualities often go hand in hand: the simplicity of an object makes it accessible to everyone, and we intuitively guess how to seize it, use it, or place it in a room. Simplicity is often a guarantee of functionality insofar as the object is stripped of all superfluous elements and designed to fulfill a given task or a role as naturally as possible. The simplicity of the design here implies a particular attention given to the forms, because it excludes the useless embellishments just as much as the rough, poorly crafted shapes of some objects, which affect their functionality. The best form thus emerges from a long quest for both simplicity and practicality. In Japan, extreme simplicity is perceived as a sign of perfection. For Masaaki Kanai, president of Ryohin Keikaku, the holding company of MUJI stores, "even the simplest Japanese tools and utensils – like the sushi knife or our everyday chopsticks – are distinguished by their extraordinary functionality."[1] Functionality extends far beyond the comfort of objects or furniture, or the ease with which we use them. It gives the users a psychic satisfaction because functional, well-designed furniture contributes to well-being.

Page 8: Mid-century pieces of furniture, with their minimalist, timeless, and functional aspect, are a good solution for decorating your home in the spirit of Japandi.

Opposite: The Japandi style favors low furniture with simple shapes, but without excessive minimalism.

Over time, the functional qualities of
the objects that surround us give them
a certain familiarity: we easily get used
to the ergonomics of a knife handle,
to the soothing light of a lamp or even
to the shape of a washbasin as long
as they meet the two criteria of simplicity
and functionality. Their use imposes
itself on us spontaneously. The concept
of "humanistic functionalism," often
associated with the work of Alvar Aalto,
can in fact be applied to the work of almost
all contemporary Japanese and Nordic
designers.

There is no antagonism between simplicity,
functionality, and elegance, since what
motivates the designers is to create
a perfect object, pleasant to the eye,
pleasant to the touch, and easy to use
and maintain. The choice of materials
and their harmonious assembly, the sense
of proportion and the harmony of colors,
are all elements that must be taken into
consideration, as well as a touch of originality
that will make the new object stand out
in the eyes of the public.

*Opposite: The repetition of square
and rectangular shapes in the decoration
of this room, including the windows, creates
a sense of ordered simplicity despite
the diversity of materials seen here: glass,
wood, textiles, metal, and painted brick.*

*Overleaf: In this living room of a
traditional Scandinavian interior, the
furniture arrangement is in the Japandi
spirit: resolutely simple, with a sofa area
subtly embellished with a rug and a coffee
table. The surrounding space allows for
free movement.*

WHAT MAKES NORDIC AND JAPANESE DESIGN TRADITIONS SO SIMILAR?

A COMMON UNDERSTANDING OF MINIMALISM

"To a Japanese, accustomed to simplicity of ornamentation and frequent change of decorative method, a Western interior permanently filled with a vast array of pictures, statuary, and bric-a-brac gives the impression of mere vulgar display of riches."

Okakura Kakuzō, *The Book of Tea*, 1906

The minimalist spirit of Japanese design and interiors, like that of the Nordic countries, has long been mistaken for a form of austerity and coldness, a reflection of a lifestyle that is, to say the least, spartan and rigorous. For those of us brought up according to the Aristotelian precept of nature fleeing emptiness and furniture perceived as a symbol of a certain social status, the sparseness that characterizes the rooms of a Japanese house or a Scandinavian home could, not so long ago, seem confusing. However, minimalism has emerged in Western culture as a major trend in design and decoration.

The idea of eliminating everything superfluous and designing objects that are durable, modest, and impervious to ephemeral fashions was first expressed in the late 1950s in the work of Dieter Rams, whose "Ten Principles for Good Design" were intended as a reaction to the "impenetrable confusion of shapes, colors, and noises" of the time. Perfection is now embodied in simple, uncluttered forms, in those best suited to the function of a particular object. The simplicity–functionality duality naturally induces a minimalist approach that is certainly not opposed to physical comfort. Everything is meant to create and maintain a feeling of tranquility. The interior space is left as empty as possible to allow the elements – air and light – and human beings to circulate without hindrance. The freedom of movement is perceived as a component of comfort in the face of an external world marked by congestion: dense crowds in the streets and on public transport, traffic jams, lines.

There is nothing superfluous in the arrangement of this bathroom. The clean shapes of the wood panels, mirror, and sink, as well as the play of light and shadow, create an atmosphere of chic minimalism.

Far from being associated with destitution, the idea of a vacuum is seen as a form of plenitude. In the words of Japanese scholar Okakura Kakuzō, "Vacuum is all potent because all containing. In vacuum alone motion becomes possible."[2]

The Japandi style, therefore, eliminates all unnecessary elements in the design of objects, and deliberately creates a space that is as empty as possible, but not uncomfortably so.

Above: Whether in the center of the living room or in a corner, the sofa and the furniture that accompanies it (coffee table, armchairs, rug) will be the focal point of the room. Everything will be arranged around them.

Opposite: Japandi minimalism invites us to reclaim the space. To regain a sense of true comfort, all unnecessary decoration should be removed.

WHEN *WABI-SABI* MEETS *HYGGE*

The unique nature of Japandi lies in the alliance of two distinct aesthetic concepts, Japanese *wabi-sabi* and Danish *hygge*, which here find a space for interaction and complementarity. Both are rooted in the traditions and lifestyles of their respective countries of origin. Each has left its mark on the local material culture to the point of becoming a kind of school of well-being and the standard of a particular way of life. But far from being incompatible, *wabi-sabi* and *hygge* mutually enrich each other by softening some excesses: the disconcerting austerity of Japanese interiors is smoothed out by the cozier side of *hygge*; and *wabi-sabi* does not restrict the choice of colors to a few very light shades, as is the case with Nordic design. Rather, the emphasis is on a play of contrasts, and on hues related to nature: earth, trees, sand, rocks, and other natural elements offer shades of color that are found in traditional interiors.

Wabi-sabi *has its philosophical origins in Zen Buddhism and in the contemplation of the order and disorder of nature. The ritual of tea drinking has contributed to the emergence of the* wabi-sabi *spirit over the centuries.*

A contemplative philosophy and an aesthetic concept: wabi-sabi

To understand the essence of *wabi-sabi*, one must remember that in Japan all things, even the most seemingly insignificant, have a soul. The cultural distinction between animate beings and inanimate objects that has governed Western thought since antiquity has no place in Japanese culture: trees, rocks, rivers, and all objects (even robots) have souls, just like animals and human beings. *Wabi-sabi*, as a contemplative philosophy inspired by Zen Buddhism, invites us to discover the "soul of objects." Their quality is not based on their market value, nor on the refinement of the way they are manufactured, but on their refined simplicity and their extremely modest appearance, with the small imperfections and marks of erosion that characterize objects shaped by time. Practiced as early as the 15th century by Zen monk Murata Jukō, *wabi-sabi* took off a century later, propagated by tea merchants and masters of tea who freed themselves from the frantic race for luxury deployed in the ritual surrounding the tea ceremony to bring the drink itself back to its central role, as it had almost become incidental. One of the most famous theorists of *wabi-sabi*, Sen no Rikyū (1522–1591), had a tea pavilion for one of his wealthy patrons built as a replica of a humble peasant hut.

Above: The admiration of what is ephemeral and what has stood the test of time is at the heart of wabi-sabi.

Pages 26–27: Hygge could be defined as "the little extra touch of comfort" that softens life: cushions, a warm blanket, a houseplant, and a few carefully chosen decorative objects are essential elements.

Rather than encouraging us to admire the perfection of smooth, flawless objects, *wabi-sabi* emphasizes the connection between objects and nature: as architect and critic Leonard Koren, one of the best Western connoisseurs of the philosophy, points out, *wabi-sabi* banishes all decoration that is not an integral part of the structure, for "'material poverty, spiritual richness' are *wabi-sabi* bywords."[3] Imperfection is perceived here as a spiritual supplement, not as an anomaly, because it invites a special relationship, tactile or visual, with the material that makes up the objects. Organic and soft shapes are favored on account of their resemblance to natural forms.

If simplicity is at the heart of the *wabi-sabi* philosophy, the purity of the lines should not imply an excessive minimalism, which is often synonymous with sterility. The main idea is to eliminate anything in excess and just to enjoy what is essential. As Leonard Koren stresses, "*wabi-sabi* is exactly about the delicate balance between the pleasure we get from things and the pleasure we get from freedom of things."[4]

"Material poverty, spiritual richness."

Cozy comfort in the pursuit of true happiness: hygge

The recent craze for Danish *hygge* and its Swedish equivalent, *lagom,* has made these notions familiar to all those in search of more comfort, even if *hygge* is still too often narrowed down to a form of cocooning on long winter evenings. The underlying idea of *hygge* goes far beyond that: the objects that surround us and the interior design can contribute to our well-being and provide a sense of peace that is ideal for relaxation. *Hygge* should be understood as a soft therapy: the interior of a home forms a protective bulwark against the noise and agitation to which we are exposed daily. This small and cozy nest invites us to rest and restore our strength and helps us avoid the physical and psychological exhaustion that threatens many urban dwellers. Everything must be designed to encourage rest: the choice of soft, warm colors, the lighting (several indirect light sources are better than a central ceiling light), the choice of furniture with simple, rounded shapes, and the materials (preferably of natural origin) are all factors to be considered for enjoying life. Conviviality is an important part of the *hygge* philosophy: a large table, made of wood, for sharing moments with friends and a sofa where the whole family can curl up are essential elements.

Nothing sets *wabi-sabi* in opposition to *hygge*. In different ways, both help us admire the real beauty and harmony around us and enjoy quiet moments. The importance of floral decoration in *wabi-sabi* and *hygge* emphasizes the essential role played by nature in both cases, and even more so in the Japandi style: natural materials, organic forms, and indoor plants are essential.

Living in harmony with nature, and if possible close to it, is a common denominator of both Japanese and Nordic lifestyles. It is one of the hallmarks of Japandi.

SOFT AND HARMONIOUS COLORS

In Nordic design, light and brightness, in addition to nature, play an essential role. The low light levels in the winter months encourage interior designers to use white in all its shades in the design of spaces to retain as much light as possible. More than any other color, white reflects light rather than absorbing it. Natural light is provided by windows and glass doors, and artificial light sources such as lamps are arranged to provide a soft, relaxing light. The reputation of Scandinavian designers in the field of lighting is rooted in the need to optimize the use of light. Favoring white does not mean imposing a monochrome uniformity: an entire palette of shades is used smartly to give objects and rooms a warm atmosphere and subtle contrasts: pure white can be juxtaposed with an ivory white or a creamy beige. The key here is to avoid tiring the eye and the mind by using a hue that is too intense or too strong. If darker colors are used to brighten up the interior – a blue sofa or a gray carpet, for example – the shade should be deliberately neutral to maintain the peaceful and harmonious character of the whole.

The Japanese tradition here differs from what defines the Nordic style: in Japan, the emphasis is more on colors related to nature, whether inspired by the vegetal world or the earth.

Soft but warm hues are emphasized: beige, green, terracotta, brown, and gray, often with a play of contrast between light and dark. The color enhances the space and the objects that furnish it, but it must never break the dominant minimalist and self-effacing spirit. The harmony of colors plays a central role, as the rooms must be in accordance with the peace that emanates from a well-ordered natural landscape. Here we find certain principles of *wabi-sabi*: *kanso* (simplicity), *kōko* (weathered), *shizen* (nature), and *seijaku* (tranquility). White, the color of purity and honesty in Japanese culture, may be present in the decoration, but never dominates.

Despite this difference in the use of colors and their psychological perception, the two approaches find common ground in the Japandi style: while chalky white and light shades (pale pink) are the norm, the use of natural and soft colors gives character and a touch of warmth to interiors. Contrasts with dark colors – charcoal gray, dark brown – play less with complementary colors than with the distinction of the different objects and furniture that decorate the room. The chromatic diversity is thus reconciled with the necessary harmony of interior spaces.

Try soft colors with a nice play of contrasts.

NATURE AS A MODEL AND SOURCE OF INSPIRATION

The love of nature and organic forms is a key point of convergence between Japanese designers and their Nordic counterparts. This is not surprising when one considers the importance of nature in the Nordic and Japanese lifestyles. In Sweden, free access to nature, or *allemansrätt*, is even guaranteed in the constitution. This principle, which originated in medieval customary law, is also valid in all other Nordic countries. It has kept the ancient Scandinavian bond with nature intact and undoubtedly contributes to the fact that the people of the Nordic countries see nature as a common good to be protected and respected. The "outdoor life," in other words the time one spends in contact with the forest, lakes, islands, and mountains, is a leisure activity that is taken for granted and practiced regularly. Light – the light of endless summer evenings and that of winter days when the snow illuminates the landscape more than the sun – also plays an important role in the attachment that the people of Northern Europe feel toward nature. It has also inspired many artists, including the painters of the Skagen School and of course Edvard Munch.

In an archipelago like Japan, exposed to earthquakes, tsunamis, and volcanic eruptions, the love of nature could be more nuanced than it is in the Nordic countries: nevertheless, the Japanese show a deep sensitivity to nature and to the beauty of the diverse landscapes: from the unpredictable but sublime violence of the elements to the ephemeral softness of trees in bloom, everything is a pretext for admiring the natural surroundings. Contrary to Western thought, which tends to establish a human domination over what surrounds us, Japanese thought sees in nature the origin of earthly harmony and even, according to the French geographer and philosopher Augustin Berque, "the source of social order."[5] There is as much interest in the tiny – a snowflake or the wings of a butterfly, for example – as in the beauty of a mountain or a river.

Light-colored wood is one of the signature materials of Nordic design.

A taste for natural materials

However, this deeply rooted love of nature cannot alone explain the preference for natural materials and organic forms. As we have already seen, it is the *wabi-sabi* tradition in Japan that has given value to simplicity and the use of natural materials such as wood for furniture and clay for cookware. In Scandinavia, the abundance of wood makes it an omnipresent material in everything from shipbuilding to kitchen utensils. Everything that can be produced in wood is made of it: cutlery, pitchers, chairs and stools, tables, houses, and children's games, to name just a few well-known examples. Each wooden object is unique, with its own shade and imperfections. Patina and wear add a touch of nobility to the furniture and utensils of everyday life. This is also true of ceramic objects, natural textiles, and glass.

The preference for natural materials also stems from the desire to produce durable objects from elements that, unlike synthetic materials, have not undergone industrial processing and therefore have a reduced impact on the environment. From this point of view, the Japandi spirit is perfectly in tune with the public's growing desire for eco-responsible design.

Alvar Aalto's Savoy vase, originally designed in 1936, has stood the test of time.

This undulating teak salad bowl, designed by Finnish master Finn Juhl, would fit right in with the work of a traditional Japanese craftsman.

Organic forms

While Art Nouveau in the late 19th century elevated curved lines and decorative motifs drawn from nature, it was the great names of Nordic design, primarily the Finn Alvar Aalto and the Dane Arne Jacobsen, who laid the foundations for contemporary organic design. The *Savoy* vase, designed by Aalto in 1936, has become the archetype of this movement that brings the harmony and simple beauty of nature into the modern lifestyle through objects with soft, rounded, enveloping, often asymmetrical shapes reminiscent of protozoan organisms. In choosing the name *Savoy* – which means "wave" in Finnish – for this vase, Aalto also highlighted two important themes of organic design: that of movement and undulation, and of the ephemeral, a prime motif in Japanese aesthetics. The butterfly, a fragile and fleeting creature, served as the model for the Japanese designer Sōri Yanagi's *Butterfly* stool, created in 1954, which embodies the alliance of Western influences and traditional Japanese craftsmanship. Yanagi was greatly influenced by working with Charlotte Perriand and by Le Corbusier's functionalist theories in the early 1940s, as well as by the passion of his father, Sōetsu Yanagi, a writer and the founder of the Japanese Folk Art Museum, for traditional crafts. The curves of the stool, subtle and sensual, echo the aesthetics of calligraphy while exalting a certain organic beauty dear to Japanese culture.

At the crossroads between calligraphy and organic design: the Butterfly stool by Sōri Yanagi.

Some of Sōri Yanagi's contemporaries, such as Isamu Kenmochi and Motomi Kawakami, also strove to reconcile Western influences with local craftsmanship, which enabled them to forge close ties with furniture manufacturers and department-store chains. It is not surprising, then, that Japanese craftspeople and traditional furniture brands still call on designers today to renew their collections in a style that is true to the past, in tune with the spirit of the times and the appeal of nature.

A PASSION FOR DETAIL AND SUSTAINABLE MATERIALS

The Japanese noun *shokunin* is little known in the Western world, even though it is one of the key words for understanding the spirit of Japan. *Shokunin* are craftspeople who have become masters of their profession and whose entire careers are devoted, with humility and patience, to perfecting their skills. They follow the Japanese proverb "Perfection does not consist in doing extraordinary things, but in doing ordinary things in an extraordinary way."

In the words of cabinetmaker Shuji Nakagawa, "What differentiates the work of a *shokunin* from that of an artist is that the former creates only one object, but repeated over and over again. It is not only my own experience, but that which has been passed on to me by my ancestors."[6]

Although the quest for perfection is not so theorized in Scandinavian countries, the same concern for perfect work can be found in the oeuvre of Hans J. Wegner (1914–2007). Wegner, one of the pioneers of Danish design, trained as a cabinetmaker from the age of fourteen before embarking on a career as a designer, where the skills he acquired during his apprenticeship were used to create chairs with simple, elegant, and organic forms, produced in noble types of wood, which even today have lost none of their original freshness. Wegner modestly said of his timelessly designed *501 Round Chair* (1949): "This chair could have been

created a hundred years ago – nothing new." And yet, a decade later, it embodied modernity when the young politician John F. Kennedy adopted it for his televised debate against Richard Nixon because of its rounded seat that relieved his back. Perfection in Scandinavian design is not limited to drawing clean lines: particular care is given to finishes, ergonomics, and the choice of materials. The desire to make objects that stand the test of time has led designers and manufacturers in both Japan and the Nordic countries to favor sustainable natural resources, primarily wood, but also ceramics, glass, wool, and animal skins. This is by no means an expression of nostalgia for the past, but a desire to perpetuate a unique know-how and to give it its rightful place in contemporary design.

The PP501 chair by Hans J. Wegner is an example of the "perfect object." Originally produced by Johannes Hansen, today it is in the collection of the Danish PP Møbler brand.

Lightweight and strong, bamboo is a durable natural material that is perfect for interior design.

"All materials have their own unwritten laws ... One should never be violent with a material one is working with, and the designer should seek to be in harmony with his material."

Tapio Wirkkala (1915–1985), Finnish designer and sculptor

CHAPTER 2

An insight into the studios:
30 characteristically Japandi
design objects and
their creators

OEO STUDIO COPENHAGEN (DENMARK)

ANNE-MARIE BUEMANN AND THOMAS LYKKE

OEO Studio, founded in 2003 by Anne-Marie Buemann and Thomas Lykke in Copenhagen, nowadays runs a second office in Tokyo and has developed creative partnerships with Japanese artisans and manufacturers. To define their aesthetic vision, the two founders coined the concept of *compelling minimalism*, which includes simple shapes, a focus on natural materials, and a passion for the tiniest details, in line with Japandi style. Since 2012, the designers have been working with a group of Kyoto-based artisans under the Japan Handmade label to create modern objects using traditional techniques, such as the *Harmony* tea set and the *Ki-oke* stool. The studio's prolific portfolio also includes design objects for brands such as Danish manufacturer Brdr. Krüger and Leica Camera in Japan, as well as interior design for Michelin-starred restaurants, cafés, showrooms, and residential interiors.

FIVE QUESTIONS FOR THOMAS LYKKE

What do you think are the most significant similarities between Japanese and Danish design traditions?
I believe that there is a shared appreciation for quality and attention to detail, combined with a high notion of aesthetics and simplicity. Both cultures have an almost humble and more austere approach to design. Neither Japanese nor Danish design is flashy or opulent in style, but more grounded and deeper.

Which Japanese design objects and craftsmanship traditions have particularly impressed you and influenced your own design aesthetic?
It is difficult to pick just a few since there are many interesting craftsmanship traditions still thriving in Japan, from paper to cast iron, textiles, wood, brooms, lacquerware, and ceramics, to name but a few. If you dig deep enough, these traditions are equally interesting and fascinating in the hands of skilled craftspeople. Yet areas that we have been more privileged to explore include pottery, textiles, wood, metal knitting, tea caddies, bamboo crafts, and *tenugui* (thin cotton hand towels). All mind-blowing traditions, and we feel honored and humble to have been invited in. One craft that has always fascinated me and which we have not yet explored is that of sword-making (*katana*) – a truly fascinating process with many different skills involved.

What in your experience of working with Japanese artisans and designers has struck you most about the way they work?
They share a passion, deep respect, and honor that is best described as a way of life. It feels like they become one with their skills and craft.

One of your biggest successes has been bringing attention to Japanese design by putting Japan Handmade, a collective of six Kyoto-based companies, onto the map of the international design world. How can embracing their work be an eye-opening experience for contemporary designers in the West?
We have been extremely privileged in being able to build very deep relations in Japan over the years. Creating the brand collaborative Japan Handmade (in Japan, referred to as GOON), with six crafts companies with different skill sets and very different backgrounds, has been one of the most personal and rewarding projects we have done. Japan Handmade has almost become a superhero role model for a new generation of designers and craftspeople.

Do you see the Japandi style developing as a complementary trend to Nordic and Japanese designs?
That is a good question. We do not believe so much in trends in general since they are short-lived. I think the shared values and similarities already touched upon in the first question will continue, in which case I guess my answer would be yes.

Harmony porcelain collection, 2012
OEO Studio, Copenhagen & Asahiyaki Pottery, Uji

The *Harmony* collection of porcelain objects was created
by the OEO studio team in partnership with the Asahiyaki
kiln, a pottery workshop with a 400-year history, which is
particularly famous for its tea sets. The collection consists
of three trays of various sizes, cups, a teapot, and vases
with rounded and organic yet highly functional forms. The
traditional elements of the tea ceremony are thus reinvented
with a sense of loyalty to the Japanese spirit, yet with a *hygge*
note, focused on well-being and the cozy feeling provided by
a tea-drinking session. The objects in the collection are all
two-toned, with mixtures of black and dark blue, black, and
light gray, or black and pale pink. Thus, the unity of style and
appearance avoids the pitfall of uniformity. Each object has
its own distinctive touch: together, the pieces of the collection
form a symphony of calming colors.

Ki-oke stool, 2012
OEO Studio and Nakagawa Mokkougei

To create this stool with its elegant, rounded shapes, the designers at OEO teamed up with a Japanese master of *ki-oke* (wooden buckets), cabinetmaker Nakagawa Mokkougei, the descendant of a dynasty of craftsmen specializing in wooden products. Depending on their size, these traditional buckets can be used for bathing rituals or for various domestic purposes such as storing rice or miso. The *ki-oke* is an object whose use in Japan dates back to the dawn of time, and its manufacture follows an ancestral technique whose use has been attested for more than 700 years. Each of the wooden slats that make up the *ki-oke* is connected to adjacent pieces by bamboo dowels discreetly inserted into the thickness of the slat. The arrangement is such that the whole appears to be made of one piece; no joints are visible to the naked eye. The wood species used are Japanese cypress (*sawara*) or Japanese lignified cedar (*jindai-sugi*) with a natural patina of 2000 years. Metal strips on the outside ensure the solidity of the whole. A handmade *ki-oke* has a life span of several decades. The base of the stool is shaped like a *ki-oke*. It is covered with a slightly curved seat that is very comfortable. Simplicity, functionality, and love of detail combine in this extremely light stool, which will find its place in an entrance hall or, even better, in a bathroom.

The Japanese lignified cedar edition is limited, and all the pieces are numbered. The stool is now in the permanent collections of the Victoria and Albert Museum in London and the Musée des Arts Décoratifs in Paris.

ANDERSSEN & VOLL OSLO (NORWAY)

TORBJØRN ANDERSSEN AND ESPEN VOLL

Since 2009, the Norwegian design duo Torbjørn Anderssen and Espen Voll have made their mark on furniture and tableware design. They have worked with brands such as Magis and Muuto and have won several international awards such as the Red Dot Design Award and the Wallpaper Design Award. While they draw their inspiration from the Scandinavian design tradition, the pair do not hesitate to take some liberties and to allow for a certain originality, as their aim is to create objects with innovative shapes: "We're quite open. We start designing and watch a piece take on its own personality. It's almost like breathing life into it," they state. In addition to their partnership with the Japanese brand Ariake, which resulted in the *Saga* stool, Anderssen and Voll have created a line of kitchen utensils directly inspired by their experience of everyday objects in Japan.

Saga stool, 2017
Torbjørn Anderssen and Espen Voll for Ariake

The brand Ariake ("daybreak" in Japanese) was born from
a partnership between two furniture manufacturers based
in Saga, southwestern Japan. The brand's aim is to offer
high-end furniture, created by a team of designers pairing
young Japanese talent with creators from Nordic countries.
The emphasis is on natural materials, with a predominance
of wood (oak, ash, hinoki, cedar).

The *Saga* stool, designed by Torbjørn Anderssen and Espen
Voll, is characterized by its curved seat in the shape
of an enlarged ellipse, relatively common in Japan,
which rests on a light but very stable rectangular frame.
The resolute minimalism of the lines does not affect
the comfort of the stool.

Sagyo table, 2017
Keiji Ashizawa for Ariake

A perfect companion to the *Saga* stool, *Sagyo*, by designer
Keiji Ashizawa, is a small table, delicately crafted with a narrow
top and raised edge. The table is supported by four rectangular
legs, with the front ones set on a diagonal. Its light structure
makes it suitable for use as a side desk in a living room or as
a dressing table in a bedroom. Two accessories – a small shelf
and a mirror – can be added as magnetic attachments.

AKIKO KEN MADE KOKKEDAL (DENMARK)

AKIKO KUWAHATA AND KEN WINTHER

Living in a spacious villa north of Copenhagen, Akiko Kuwahata and Ken Winther perfectly embody the complementarity and interaction of Japanese and Danish designs. After studying design at Nihon University in Tokyo, Akiko trained as a cabinetmaker, first in Japan and then at the Aarhus School of Architecture in Denmark. Ken, born into a family of cabinetmakers, followed the family tradition by joining PP Møbler, a Danish brand highly respected for the quality of its furniture, before studying with renowned craftsmen during visits to Japan. In their home workshop, Akiko and Ken create objects from sketches to finished products, constantly striving to push the boundaries of what can be designed with wood, in a creative dialogue in which the culture of each country and their personal experiences play important roles.

FIVE QUESTIONS FOR AKIKO KUWAHATA AND KEN WINTHER

What, in your opinion, are the most striking similarities between Japanese and Danish design traditions?
Simplicity above all can be the headline. Both design cultures are very pure, and anything redundant is eradicated. It is understood not as a sign of poverty but rather of rich simplicity. Often the materials are allowed to speak their own language.
What is interesting is that the Japanese design tradition is very old and has been refined over 1000 years or so, whereas the Danish design culture developed from the 1920s to the 1970s and continues with the design of today. And these two approaches work very well together, or fit each other very well.

Would you define your work as a fusion of Japanese and Danish designs, or is it just the expression of your own style?
We don't seek fusion. It is, as you mention in your question, just the expression of our style. It comes from within us. We have great respect for each other, and for our cultural differences, through our collaboration. When we create new work, it is somehow in our blood.

How do the two of you complement each other in your working process?
Normally, Akiko gets various ideas, then we do some sketching together. Then Akiko continues the ideas, making small models in cardboard. Ken, as a craftsman, brings in what is possible to do with wood. When we do the sketching, we don't think about what is doable or not – we just free our minds. If the design requires it, we like to take up the challenge – where can we push ourselves and the wood further. After the first few sketches, we don't hesitate and just go to the workshop to craft a quick, full-scale mockup. Here, as is often

the case with our sketches, we discover the design and which way we want to go. Our whole process resembles a game of ping-pong.

How important is it to you to create all your beautiful designs from scratch? Is it just perfectionism that has led you to this choice, or the feeling of keeping traditions of craftsmanship alive?
Akiko is a designer and Ken is a cabinetmaker. We have both skills in-house, so to speak. We are unusual in that we can design and make products ourselves. Today, however, we have some of our designs in production by other manufacturers, so it is not particularly sacred for us.

You have specialized in design objects made of wood. In your opinion, which qualities make wood so valuable to contemporary designers?
Wood is a common material that has been used since time immemorial. It still has new possibilities – new ways in which it can be used. And when you refine your process and craftsmanship, wood will reveal even more of its beauty. Furthermore, wood is a very tactile material, and if you encounter well-shaped wood it is often irresistible; you can't help but touch it with your hands.

Wooden curtain
Akiko Kuwahata and Ken Winther

Designed for the Michelin-starred restaurant Inua in Tokyo, this curtain made of wooden slats can be hung to soften the light from a bay window, or can be used as a semi-transparent screen to divide a space and create a more intimate atmosphere. The intertwined slats of Oregon pine create a moiré effect that adds to the magic of this delicate, elegant, and functional construction.

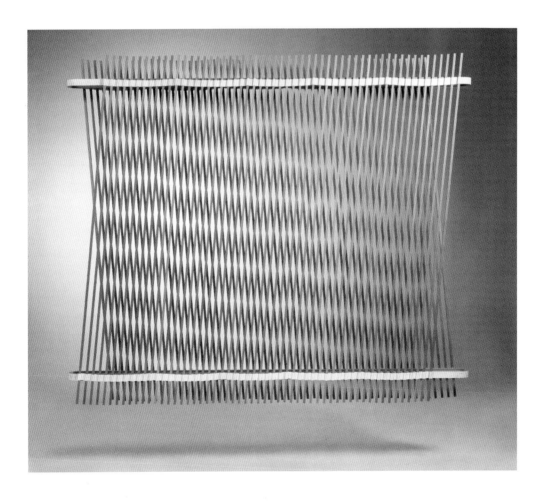

Carousel jewelry box
Akiko Kuwahata and Ken Winther

When closed, the *Carousel* jewelry box is hardly distinguishable
from other boxes of the same type, although its tinted
Plexiglas lid invites curiosity. The true genius of the box lies
in the pretty central cone, around which rings can be laid. The
tip of the cone is used to hold the lid in position, and allows
the boxes to be stacked on top of one another, making them
easy to store vertically. For added visual appeal, the jewelry box
is available in three types of wood: walnut, cherry, and maple,
with pale-pink, turquoise, and snow-white lids. Simplicity,
functionality, elegance, and love of detail – this is the epitome
of Japandi style.

Facet coffee table
Akiko Kuwahata and Ken Winther

The same interest in the effects of light, shadow, and movement is evident in the design of the *Facet* coffee table. "A monochrome object exposed to light and shadow reveals an endless range of colors, as the light strikes a new facet from a new angle," explain Akiko and Ken. In this case, "the shadow takes on a slightly darker note with every new facet it encounters." The oval tabletop of glass also plays a part in the constant interplay between brightness and shadow by reflecting light into the inner part of the table. We are thus invited to admire the ephemeral passage of light rays on the wood and the delicate nuances of color.

Breathe chest of drawers
Akiko Kuwahata and Ken Winther

Is it the glass structure that gives this chest of drawers
a sense of lightness? Or is it the four slim, tapered legs?
This lightness is reminiscent of Japanese houses with their
sliding *shoji* doors. This piece of furniture is unpretentious in its
appearance but magical in its effect. When one of the chest's
side drawers opens or closes, the opaque stripes that decorate
the glass panels and the grooves of the wooden drawers –
whose stripes are arranged in the opposite direction to the
panels' lines – interact with one another to form an illusion of
movement. The chest reveals small translucent openings that
invite you to play with the drawers, to let air and light into the
heart of the piece, a bit like taking a breath.

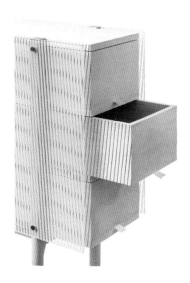

STUDIOA27

LARS VEJEN, AARHUS (DENMARK) AND TAIJIRO ISHIKO, KYOTO (JAPAN)

While maintaining their respective practices in Aarhus and Kyoto, designers Lars Vejen and Taijiro Ishiko have founded studioA27, a joint venture for the projects they create together. The combination of traditional craft techniques and technological innovation is a hallmark of all work by studioA27. Among other projects, Vejen and Ishiko have designed a line of furniture for the Japanese manufacturer Hirata, the *Hirata Gen Collection*, and a kit that includes a traditional notebook, binder cord, and bag for T.S.BRAND. The designers also participated in a renovation and interior-design project for a villa in Kyoto.

Float chair, 2019
Lars Vejen and Taijiro Ishiko

The *Float* chair is the first project that was co-signed by
Lars Vejen and Taijiro Ishiko. It is a quintessential example
of Japandi principles: at once functional and elegant, it draws
the eye in with its pure form and simplicity. Like the seat,
the oak backrest, in a natural or black color, is placed on a
curved metal tube and seems to float delicately in the air. The
seat is comfortable and the structure light enough to be lifted
with one hand. Classic but with a touch of originality, like all
objects designed by Vejen, as well as nicely proportioned, the
chair offers a perfect balance between the softness of wood
and the hardness of metal.

Hirata Gen Collection, 2020
Lars Vejen and Taijiro Ishiko

For this collection of eighteen different pieces of furniture, the designers at studioA27 partnered with the Hirata Chair factory, a family-owned wooden furniture company founded in 1963 in Morodomi (Saga Prefecture), one of the cradles of Japanese woodworking. The spirit of the collection is contained in the word *gen* (meaning "gene" in Danish, "origin" in Japanese): the designers' wish was to create furniture pieces that would share the same basic features while reflecting a certain diversity of forms, and to make use of handicraft techniques and natural materials such as wood and traditionally tanned leather. All the furniture is assembled by hand by Shoji Hirata's team with unparalleled care. The clean, minimalist lines, with great attention to the finishing touches, do not prevent you from feeling at ease. The sofa and the armchair are available in three variations, depending on the height of the backrest, to offer various degrees of privacy. Similarly, the round table is available in several heights and diameters to suit the needs of each room. The daybed can be equipped with small circular side tables, as can the sofa and the armchair.

Functionality is at the heart of the collection. The stools have handles, the chairs are easily stacked, and a circular side table or tray can be added to the corner of the sofa or the daybed.

DESIGN STUDIO
LARS VEJEN AARHUS (DENMARK)

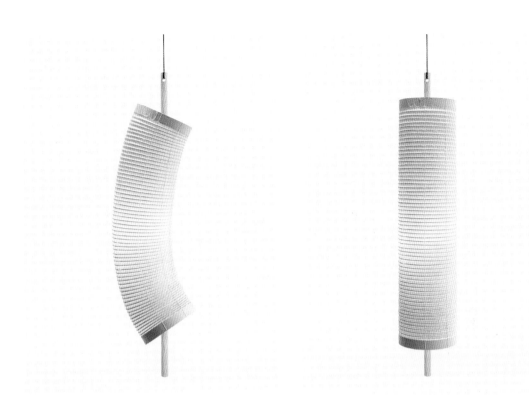

Stick lantern lamp, 2017
Lars Vejen

Lars Vejen has undertaken solo collaborations with Japanese artisans. Among other items, he designed a lantern lamp, *Stick*, for the family business Kobishiya Chube in Kyoto by adapting the aesthetic of the paper-and-bamboo lamp to Western taste. The light structure of this model, with its flexible form, is supported by wooden rods that run through its center and allow it to hang vertically or to curve. The paper lamp, a symbol of East Asia, is reinvented here in an innovative look and with a modern touch. Its soft, relaxing light is perfect for a bedroom or living room, or as an accent lamp in a small room with natural light.

EN modular vase, 2017
Lars Vejen

To create this adjustable and distinctively contoured vase,
Lars Vejen partnered with the Asada Kawara workshop,
the only manufacturer in Kyoto still handcrafting traditional
decorative tiles. The exceptional quality of the clay and the
preservation of ancient techniques have contributed to making
Asada Kawara an exemplar of artisanal craftsmanship. The
different elements that comprise the vase can easily be
assembled and adjusted to the size of the plants forming
the decoration. Elegant and understated, the modular vase
highlights the flowers and stems that escape from the matte
clay structure through small openings.

HIROMICHI KONNO TOKYO (JAPAN)

Hiromichi Konno studied product design in both Japan and Sweden. His work celebrates numerous common features of Scandinavian and Japanese traditions, whose influences are harmoniously fused in his designs of everyday objects. Enchanted during childhood by his grandmother folding origami, Konno has always taken a hands-on approach. An appreciation of nature, a limited color palette, excellent craftsmanship, and sensual forms, as well as a sense of energy, are among the main features of his work. The *process of form finding*, as the designer describes his method of developing new projects, is carefully thought through and unhurried in search of the perfect final result. Since 2002 the designer has been based in Tokyo. In addition to developing his own projects, often in collaboration with Scandinavian manufacturers, Konno supervises other design brands, and runs workshops for children. Through this multifaceted practice, the designer says his aim is to find an ideal vision of design for the future.

THREE QUESTIONS FOR HIROMICHI KONNO

During your studies at the Chiba Institute of Technology in Japan you went on your first trip abroad to Copenhagen. What led you to choose Scandinavia?
I was already studying and had some knowledge of Scandinavian design by the time I first visited Copenhagen. So I thought I should experience it and see it for myself. I also wanted to discover the reasons why such designs were created in Scandinavia. I thought there must be interesting stories behind them.

After this trip you decided to continue studying in Scandinavia, specifically at the Umeå Institute of Design (UID) in Sweden. What further impressions of Nordic aesthetics did you gain?
More than all the education I received in Sweden, it is what I have gained from everyday life that has had most impact on me as a designer. A long, dark winter seems very inconvenient in many ways, but it is one of the major sources of inspiration for Scandinavian design. The climate, temperature of the air, color of the sky and sea ... everything is reflected in the objects created, and people in Scandinavia are very good at making winter enjoyable.

What makes Japanese and Scandinavian design traditions a harmonious match, and which aspects of both aesthetics are particularly important to you?
Both Japan and Scandinavia tend to give much importance to "hospitality," I believe. And there is also a long history of designing for "everyday life," rather than for "social status." I am more than willing to inherit this tradition, and treasure the essence of it. Hopefully it will somehow reach our next generation and those that follow.

CHAT sofa, 2009
Hiromichi Konno for Softline

This sculptural sofa is made of only two elements – a simple base with a rounded backrest sitting lightly on top – and is somewhat reminiscent of a Zen rock garden. The organic inspiration is expressed in a very minimalist yet elegant manner. At the core of this refined simplicity, the designer was aiming for coziness, an essential element in Scandinavian design, with the inviting, curvaceous back support occupying one of the corners. The designer's goal was to create the ideal arrangement for sitting down for a chat – which explains the name. Introducing natural forms into an interior, Konno achieves a perfect balance between function and aesthetics.

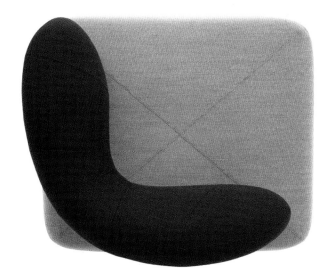

CLAESSON KOIVISTO RUNE STOCKHOLM (SWEDEN)

MÅRTEN CLAESSON, EERO KOIVISTO, AND OLA RUNE

A love of Japan and its culture is in the DNA of the architecture and design studio founded in 1995 in Stockholm by Mårten Claesson, Eero Koivisto, and Ola Rune. This helps explain the impressive collection of Japanese handicrafts and design objects gathered within its walls. These objects testify to the importance of Japan in the minds of the founders; all three had the opportunity to study there in the early 1990s and subsequently carried out design projects in the country. As Mårten Claesson likes to point out, "In the West, I think that there is a sort of rivalry between people who want to preserve traditional cultures and those who want to be creative and influence new cultures. In Japan, you don't have this kind of conflict. The different cultures are just allowed to exist side by side. The Japanese really take care of their traditions and all of their handicrafts, and at the same time they're the most technologically advanced country on Earth. They refine everything to the highest quality, which is just heaven for me as a designer and architect." The objects designed by the studio for the Japanese market, or those that are inspired by Japanese culture, number in the dozens. These include the *Kanpai* sake set (2003), the *Sha Bo* shampoo bottle (2004), the *Ceremony* tea set (2013), the *Matsumoto* chair (2016), and *Tsubaki* bowls (2018). The studio has also constructed several buildings in Japan.

Soya coffee table, 2011
Claesson Koivisto Rune

The *Soya* coffee table is loosely based on the small plates
used in Japan to mix soy sauce with wasabi for dipping sushi
and sashimi. Its slightly asymmetrical contours recall the petals
of a flower. The white veins in the Marquina marble give each
table a unique and natural look in the spirit of *wabi-sabi*.
The table is also available in white Carrara marble with gray
veins that brighten its surface.

Hand table, bench, and stool, 2019
Claesson Koivisto Rune

The trio of designers was invited to contribute to an art initiative, Tokyo Craft Room, and they teamed up with master carpenter Yuji Takahashi to develop the *Hand* furniture collection, consisting of a table, bench, and stool. Made of wood – locally sourced Hiroshima chestnut – the set was envisioned with a focus on shapes and solutions that would be possible to achieve only with the use of hand tools. The perfect proportions of the convex forms and the absence of right angles highlight the wood's natural texture, which makes the set very tactile, with small imperfections that are invisible yet perceptible through touch. Masterfully crafted, the furniture appears light but at the same time has mass. This is also thanks to the delicate four-millimeter joints designed to give the impression of the wood being loosely stacked. They protrude through the surfaces to firmly connect all elements. Takahashi studied wood joinery (*sashimono*) to make robust pieces of furniture that are long-lasting and repairable.

Objet d'art n° 2, 2018
Claesson Koivisto Rune for Time & Style

Using oak sourced from Hokkaido, a region famous for high-quality timber, Claesson Koivisto Rune designed this noble and minimalistic book stand. It was created for Time & Style, a Japanese furniture brand whose factory is in Asahikawa, a city where the climate is suitable for wood drying and manufacturing. To give traditional techniques a modern twist, the designers used contemporary, clean shapes. Two juxtaposed planes are stripped to the essential, so that the book stand becomes invisible while fulfilling its role. Crafted to last, this basic form is a perfect canvas for the coarse pattern of the wood grain.

"I feel that the furniture is both Scandinavian and Japanese at the same time. We can't get away from our Scandinavian background, but there's something Japanese about the shapes. They have a cuteness ... soft and friendly, yet super precise."

Mårten Claesson

Furniture from the Claesson Koivisto Rune collection.

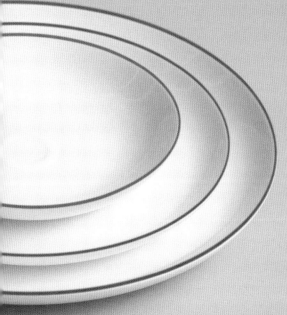

Hibito tableware collection, 2019
Cecilie Manz for Actus

This sophisticated set, designed for the Japanese brand Actus, juxtaposes various materials that have a mutually enhancing power: white porcelain from Arita, stainless-steel cutlery from Niigata, bamboo from Kyūshū, and traditional glass, as well as kimono textiles. According to Manz's vision, Danish design is about sensibility toward materiality, and the key is to use the right material in the right place. The *Hibito* collection is a celebration of craftsmanship and quality in functional objects for everyday use. The subtly rounded, simple shapes bring to mind the ephemeral ripples on the surface of disturbed water.

Osaka furniture collection, 2020
Teruhiro Yanagihara for Offecct

"I design interiors, and I always think about the space," says
Teruhiro Yanagihara. With the *Osaka* collection, the designer
aimed to use the furniture to create a landscape. Inspired
by Japanese gardens filled with stones, moss, and trees,
the collection includes six different designs – three tables and
three ottomans. Reduced to pure geometric forms, the pieces
are an expression of purity, with frames made of plywood
and solid wood covered with cold-glued foam. The smoothly
sanded edges give the shapes an organic feel, enhanced by
the texture of the upholstery fabric. "The elements of the
Osaka collection are like reflections of one another, jigsaw
pieces that can be combined in different ways," explains
the manufacturer.

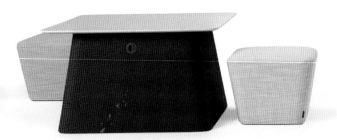
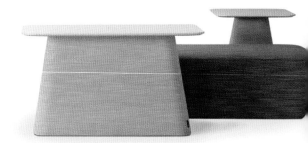

TERUHIRO YANAGIHARA
KOBE (JAPAN) AND ARLES (FRANCE)

Teruhiro Yanagihara studied architecture and founded his practice in 2002, "to develop his own, identifiable vision of design." Working with both Japanese and international brands, Yanagihara blurs the boundaries between Eastern and Western aesthetics by blending the formal language of contemporary design with Japanese crafts. He tends to fuse traditional and innovative elements. Yanagihara's work demonstrates a successful mixture of modern technologies with Japanese spirituality. His style can be described as *poetic minimalism*, with a strong sense of materials and a restricted color palette. His goal is to design something timeless and ubiquitous. Known for creating objects as well as for commercial interiors, Yanagihara previously worked as artistic director of the furniture brand Karimoku New Standard and is now active in the same position at 1616/Arita Japan, a four-century-old pottery manufacturer. He envisioned the *Osaka* collection for Offecct as a new narrative, with the intention of creating a new connection between Japan and Scandinavia.

STILLEBEN COPENHAGEN (DENMARK)

DITTE RECKWEG AND JELENA SCHOU NORDENTOFT

Ditte Reckweg and Jelena Schou Nordentoft, the founders of Stilleben, studied design at the Royal Danish Academy of Fine Arts and chose to specialize in glass and ceramic work. They founded Stilleben in 2002 with the aim of creating objects with clean lines and timeless elegance, yet which are deeply rooted in craft traditions: objects that are perfectly adapted to contemporary lifestyles and of excellent quality. In the same spirit, they subsequently opened a design boutique where their own creations are artistically displayed with those of other carefully selected designers. In addition to glass and ceramics, their portfolio now extends to textiles and interior design. The duo also work for other well-known Danish brands.

Ditte and Jelena share a passion for Japanese culture. Many of their collections are directly inspired by their memories of travel. Their extensive knowledge of Japanese design has strengthened their desire to create simple, functional everyday objects of unquestionable aesthetic value.

Yoko tea set
Ditte Reckweg and Jelena Schou Nordentoft for Motarasu

Produced for the Motarasu brand in partnership with Lyngby Porcelæn, the *Yoko* tea set includes a teapot, pitcher, and cup, all monochrome, but each available in two different hues. The Japanese female name Yoko was chosen by the designers for this service with its round, deliberately simple shapes, where two sharp decorative elements – the spouts of the teapot and the pitcher – add a distinctive touch. The polished, shiny surface of the objects clearly refers to the traditional Japanese lacquer varnish made from urushi sap. The limited number of pieces in this service seems to be in keeping with the *wabi-sabi* spirit, which invites one to focus on the ritual and the tasting of tea rather than on the opulence of the objects.

TSUKASA GOTO MILAN (ITALY)

In 2004, after studies at Salesian Polytechnic in Tokyo and at the University of Art and Design in Nagoya, Japanese designer Tsukasa Goto decided to move to Milan, where he initiated collaborations with artists, designers, and architects. Six years later, Goto started developing personal projects for various brands in both Europe and Japan in the spirit of a fusion of Eastern and Western cultures. A great sense of materials and textures characterizes his designs. Through numerous experiments, Goto aims to explore the potential of very diverse materials, such as wood, marble, cement, and metal, in pursuit of their intrinsic possibilities. His "research and development, which he calls 'facendo,' leads to the creation of unique sculptural pieces, which serve as references for production on an industrialized scale," explains EO, a Copenhagen-based brand offering a twist on Scandinavian aesthetics. Goto and EO teamed up to create the beautiful *SO* table.

SO table, 2014
Tsukasa Goto for EO

In Japanese, *sō* means "layers." The reference here is to the marks of passing time visible in the travertine tabletop and to the layers of the bent limewood frame. The designer, with a strikingly honest approach to both materials, directs our attention to the pattern of the stone and to the wood fibers in order to celebrate their tactile qualities. To put their materiality on display, Goto envisioned an object of everyday use with simple and soft lines. Characteristic of the Japanese aesthetic, the table looks quite light and airy despite its rather significant size and the use of travertine, while its oval shape and natural color palette enhance its organic character.

DESIGN STUDIO KAKSIKKO HELSINKI (FINLAND)

SALLA LUHTASELA AND WESLEY WALTERS

Salla Luhtasela and Wesley Walters met while studying at the Aalto School of Arts, Design, and Architecture in Helsinki. Their shared interest in functional objects with simple forms and natural materials led them to specialize in ceramic tableware and wooden furniture, two areas for which their studio, Kaksikko, has become renowned in Finland. Wesley Walters spent five years in Japan. He studied design at Tama Art University in Tokyo and also Japanese, which he speaks fluently. His years of learning in the Land of the Rising Sun have shaped his aesthetic vision.

Korematsu chair
Design Studio Kaksikko

Developed by design duo Salla Luhtasela and Wesley Walters
for a Japanese osteopathic practice, the *Korematsu* chair
celebrates the simple beauty of wood. The design offers
a perfect balance between the straight lines of the elongated
legs and the curves of the seat and back rails. The rails form
a crescent moon for better back support, while the curved seat
ensures optimal comfort despite the relative hardness of the
wood. The chair's uncluttered look places it at the crossroads
between design and craftsmanship, which is very much in the
spirit of Japandi.

NORM ARCHITECTS COPENHAGEN (DENMARK)

Norm Architects was established by Katrine Goldstein and Jonas Bjerre-Poulsen in 2008. The studio's activities embrace a wide range of projects spanning industrial design, architecture, interiors, and creative direction. The team's style aims at striking the right balance between richness and restraint, order, and complexity – but they also quite successfully blend aesthetics and functionality. To achieve this complex goal, they work with a muted color palette and natural materials, while clean lines define their visual language. As their objects and spaces are stripped to their simplest forms, it is the exquisite finish and haptic qualities of the rich textures they create that enhance the powerful *less is more* effect. The studio's approach, based on minimalism and Zen-inspired notions, is not only comprehensive but also very consistent across their practice. "We respect our context and build on the traditions of Scandinavian design – of timeless aesthetics, natural materials, and upholding Modernist principles of restraint and refinement," they explain.

The collection designed for Karimoku, one of Japan's leading wooden furniture manufacturers, is a fusion of the coziness and warmth cherished in Scandinavian aesthetics and the elegance and lightness specific to the Japanese tradition. All designs in the *Karimoku Case Study* collection are crafted from materials sourced from nature, and celebrate rich textures, which, though diverse, interplay beautifully with one another. This tailor-made series was developed for the renovation of the 36-unit Kinuta Terrace apartments in Tokyo by Norm Architects and the Keiji Ashizawa Design team.

N-CC01 club chair
Norm Architects for Karimoku, *Karimoku Case Study*

Comfort is at the core of the *N-CC01* club chair. The design
offers embracing curves and perfect proportions between
the softly upholstered seat, the backrest, and the shell
executed in light wood for "a more crisp, architectural, and
crafted expression," as Norm Architects emphasize. A well-
balanced combination of light wood, curvaceous shapes,
and comfortable cushions creates a feeling of warmth. The
designers show a great eye for detail in the subtle overhang
of the upholstery along the C-shaped back support continuing
into the armrests: it is a practical solution for ease of moving
the chair around, just like the chair's light structure, which
occupies little space.

N-DC01 dining chair
Norm Architects for Karimoku, *Karimoku Case Study*

"The dining chair was born out of the exploration around Karimoku's many factories, workshopping on site with the craftsmen, using existing parts and updating others, until a hybrid between the Japanese and Scandinavian design aesthetics emerged," explains the manufacturer. This dining chair showcases the mastery of Japanese craftsmanship. Simple yet refined, the oak structure is characterized by lines devoid of sharp edges. The softly curved backrest, elegant armrests, and expansive seat make it an ergonomic chair with a clear emphasis on organic forms: "Like branches of a tree, each element of the chair almost flows or grows from the others, making the chair both strong and elegant in its nature," comments the studio. Among other options, the seat is available in tightly interwoven paper cord.

Pendant light and floor and table lamps
Norm Architects for Karimoku, *Karimoku Case Study*

Norm Architects identifies minimalism with softness and
delicacy. This lighting collection, which consists of a pendant
light, a floor lamp, and a table lamp, is an homage to the
Japanese sense of aesthetics. The collection was especially
designed for the Archipelago House, a private summerhouse
in Sweden. The designs combine paper and wood in a subtle
and natural way. The conical pendant has been envisioned as a
reference to the architecture of the summerhouse and is made
of a single piece of washi paper, which is fixed to the frame
with magnets. This system facilitates disassembly of the paper
structure whenever the bulb requires replacement. The screen
covering the bottom of the cone hides the source of light
and diffuses the light in a soft and atmospheric fashion. The
standing lamps draw from the experience of Kojima Shōten,
a lantern-making workshop based in Kyoto that has been
in operation for more than two centuries. The lampshades
are also made of washi paper and are each supported by a
sculptural base, elegant and light. The idea was to design a
functional lamp that would produce a natural and indirect
light, thus contributing to a cozy atmosphere.

MOTARASU COPENHAGEN (DENMARK)

Mikkel Zebitz, the founder of Motarasu.

Pages 106–107: Design objects from the Motarasu collection on display at Izumi restaurant, Frederiksberg, Copenhagen.

Since its foundation in 2018 by Mikkel Zebitz, the Danish brand Motarasu – whose name means "to bring about change" in Japanese – has supported the emergence of Japandi style by promoting partnerships between Japanese and Scandinavian designers and craftspeople. The idea is to offer design objects that embody the aesthetic values common to both cultures: simplicity of forms, quality of finish, durability, and functionality. As its founder points out, Motarasu was born from "the meeting between two cultures, which together create a new unity."

FOUR QUESTIONS FOR MIKKEL ZEBITZ

You founded Motarasu as a platform to bring Japanese and Danish designers together. How and why did you decide to embark on this adventure?

For as long as I can remember, I have been drawn to the beauty of design and the joy it gives me. I admired the many classics from the golden age of Danish design, and like the designers, I was also fascinated by Japanese aesthetics. But it was a paradox to me that the Danes throughout time – and even more so today, for contemporary design – have looked to Japan for inspiration, but we rarely work together. I felt drawn to see what would happen if we united our efforts with the source of our inspiration.

What are the benefits of a close collaboration between designers from both countries? What, in your opinion, can Japanese designers and craftspeople offer their Danish counterparts? And how can Danish designers benefit from Japanese experience and know-how?

The Japanese have a very natural and poetic approach to design. This manifests in design through the concept of *wabi-sabi* – the embracing of the imperfect and natural as the perfect. Both in the design, where you can see, for example, that items are handcrafted in natural materials, and in the lifestyle of slowing down. So, the holistic Japanese view of life is an important source of inspiration.

Which points of convergence between the two design traditions, Japanese and Danish, do you find most striking?

Originally, the limited access to natural resources for both nations encouraged a simple focus on designs with attention to functionality, details, and craftsmanship, and this is still the case today. But I also see a common view of design through the philosophy of surrounding yourself with few objects, yet with beautiful and good-quality designs that can bring you joy.

What are the initial results and perspectives of the Motarasu brand, and how do you see the development of the Japandi style?

We are fortunate to see an increasing interest, internationally, in our designs. We feel that our mission resonates well with design lovers and that there is a growing interest in long-lasting quality and "slow design."

CHAPTER 3

Japandi style at home:
How to convert your interior
into a Japandi-inspired retreat

BEFORE YOU START

Arranging your interior in the Japandi fashion does not necessarily mean replacing all your furniture, nor sticking to an extreme minimalism that would take away all comfort and functionality from your home. Reinventing spaces, first and foremost, requires questioning what is useful and practical to you, as well as what atmosphere you want the rooms to have, and thinking about the role of light and colors.

Simplicity – and not minimalism – serves as a guideline for the Japandi style. Simplicity of form, of materials, and a sense of space are the three fundamental criteria. Let's remember that simplicity is most often a guarantee of functionality, because an object or piece of furniture with a simple form will naturally be easy to handle and maintain. Traditional materials, such as wood, bamboo, wicker, slate, ceramic, and glass, will lend a timeless aspect to the decoration and will age well. Also, nothing should encumber the space: furniture should be installed so as not to restrict movement.

Comfort, warmth, and harmony are three equally important values for creating an atmosphere in the purest spirit of Japandi. This is not limited to the choice of furniture or objects: the color of the walls and the lighting also play an essential role here. A subtle hue can bring warmth to a room and cleverly highlight the furniture with a contrasting effect. When it comes to lighting, the best option is a good balance between natural light and several properly placed lamps (rather than a central ceiling light).

And even if you don't really have a green thumb, don't forget that floral decorations and plants bring a touch of beauty and nature to an interior.

Page 108: Think Japandi, think comfort, warmth, and functionality.

Opposite: Simplicity and a sense of space are the key words for designing your interior in Japandi style.

WHEN THE ENTRANCE SETS THE TONE

One of the most common mistakes in the design of an apartment or house is to neglect the entrance, a space often reduced to a transit area between the outside world and the other rooms of the house. Its furnishings are generally restricted to the utilitarian: a coatrack, a mirror, a bench, a piece of furniture to store shoes, possibly a small chest of drawers on which to set keys or a clothes brush, a corkboard for notes and family photos. If it is true that the entrance is a place where one does not spend much time, it is nevertheless the first room of the house that guests will see. It is thus essential to give it a welcoming, functional, and aesthetic aspect, following the example of the *genkan*, the vestibule of traditional Japanese houses, where guests are welcomed into a home. A first space, around the front door, allows visitors to take off their shoes; according to the custom, they will put them with the toes facing the exit. It is also in this part of the room that guests will remove their coats. The hosts greet them from a slightly higher part of the entrance, the *yoritsuki*, which marks the interior of the house and whose decoration sets the tone: it is usually adorned with wooden panels or a *shoji* screen, and decorated with floral motifs or an element of calligraphy.

Opposite: The furniture lined up along a single wall in this bright entrance helps maximize the space. All the essentials are there: a coatrack, a stool for putting on or taking off shoes, a low chest of drawers, and a mirror.

Pages 114–15: This modern genkan, designed by OEO Studio for a residential complex in Tokyo, follows the traditional Japanese pattern, but with a sharp sense of geometric shapes and a touch of comfort (the bench along the wall).

The word *genkan* originally referred to
the entrance to a Zen temple, with all
the purification rituals that this implied.

In the Nordic countries, the entrance plays
an essential role during the long winter
months. It is the room where one warms
up after walking through the cold and snow.
The emphasis is therefore on the warm and
friendly side of the decoration, with soft
colors, lighting that adds a hint of comfort,
and furnishings that are as functional as
possible; a bench for sitting and removing
shoes is part of it (or a stool, if the space is
small). A large mirror will enlarge the room
and allow everyone to check their outfit
and hairstyle.

It is rarely possible to raise a part of the floor
to re-create the structure of the *genkan*, but
you can easily play with the surfaces: a tiled
floor can be partly covered with a rug, which
will then take on the role of the *yoritsuki*
and will offer the advantage of warming up
the room. Some thoughtful lighting will give
the entrance extra character, as will a green
plant. To add a more personal touch to
this room, you can hang a movie poster
or a watercolor to complement the mirror.

*This typically Scandinavian entrance has a large
closet for clothes. A stool and a side table complete
the simple and very practical furnishings.*

A TOUCH OF FANTASY IN THE LIVING ROOM

Let's be perfectly clear: it would be contrary to the Japandi spirit to advocate a pure minimalist style for a living room. It's a room designed for family life and friends, where everyone has a place, even pets. In the design of the living room, comfort must prevail over any other consideration, and if we had to choose only one piece of furniture that is representative of each room, the sofa would be to the living room what the bed is to the bedroom or the bathtub to the bathroom. It is therefore the choice of sofa and armchairs that will determine the atmosphere. Choose models of a reasonable size, with simple lines and in soft colors. You'll have no trouble finding armchairs and sofas with a wooden frame and seats made of natural textiles in pastel tones. Gather them around a rug and a coffee table to create a cozy island in the heart of the room. This way you will avoid dispersion and keep enough free space to facilitate circulation in the living room. Depending on the room's size, you can add other "islets," such as, for example, a small round table for drinking coffee while leafing through a magazine, or a corner with shelves where you store your books, family photos, or some beautiful objects selected with care.

Above: A pleasant living room should be filled with natural light, an essential element for our well-being.

Opposite: The living room of this house is an extension of the dining room, which facilitates the circulation between rooms.

This personal touch should be present, but always remain discreet. Lighting – preferably indirect, except of course for natural light – can add a touch of originality with lamps in simple but refined shapes, an art in which Scandinavian designers are masters. Houseplants have their place in a trendy Japandi living room, as they provide a touch of color and contribute to a relaxed atmosphere. If you like geometric shapes, a pretty cactus or succulent will do just fine.

Also, a bouquet of flowers in a pretty vase is never superfluous. For the walls, opt for a light color, such as ecru or beige, which you can combine with a darker shade to create a contrast. This second color can be that of the sofa or a shelf, to emphasize the unity of the style. If it is dark enough, it will give a certain depth to the decoration. On the floor, simplicity is best; a wooden floor or large tiles are by far the most obvious choices.

This large living room was designed by OEO Studio. Despite their impressive dimensions, the sofas do not hinder the circulation in the room. Their arrangement invites you to sit down and enjoy a moment of calm.

DINING IN A JAPANDI ATMOSPHERE

A dining room should be as warm and welcoming as possible. It's the place where you meet for dinner, where you share good food, drinks, and joyful moments with your friends; it must therefore be designed so that you feel at ease. Everything will be arranged around the table, the main piece of furniture in the room. While most tables are rectangular, a simple and practical shape, there's no reason why you can't have an oval table, made of wood or glass, with a less formal look. Well-designed wooden chairs can be very comfortable, but you can also choose leather ones, which are elegant and easy to maintain.

A warm yet muted color on the walls will help create a pleasant atmosphere, unless you decide to paint one wall in a darker hue to contrast with the rest in a neutral tone (light beige, for example). The lighting will need to be well thought out so as not to strain the eyes or make guests appear washed-out; the excessive power of a single-bulb ceiling light can have this effect, whereas a multi-lamp model will diffuse the light more evenly. Wall sconces with the right placement and brightness will enhance the entire room.

Whether oval or rectangular, the table will be the main piece of furniture in the dining room, the one around which everything will be arranged.

The furniture for a Japandi-inspired dining room can be limited to a table and chairs. However, a sideboard that will be used to store tableware, and whose top will allow you to keep some dishes at arm's length before bringing them to the table, will be very useful. Also think about floral decorations on the table and houseplants in pots, as these will give a lively character to the room.

Bright, cheerful hues, good lighting, and the presence of green plants contribute to the tranquil atmosphere of a dining room.

NOTHING SUPERFLUOUS IN THE BEDROOM

A bedroom can be designed according to the minimalist principles of Japandi and still offer a cozy, cocooning look. Simplicity and practicality do not exclude comfort or a certain warmth. If you are to feel good in it, your bedroom must reflect your personality. Even more than the rest of the house, it is the place where your personal tastes can be expressed: wall color, choice of bed, furniture, lighting; everything must contribute to your comfort and well-being.

Let's start with the walls: why not choose your favorite color? In a light, neutral shade, obviously. If you like beige, blue, gray, pink, purple, or green, that's not a problem. The task is a little more difficult if you dream of a room in red or black, but nothing is impossible: for red, review the variations of orange-red, soft enough to suit a room dedicated to rest and relaxation. Decorating all the walls of a room in black is quite unusual, unless you can sleep only in total darkness, but painting a section of wall in this color to form a contrast with a much lighter area can be a good idea. It's an original way to give the room a little character. Another possibility, wooden panels, would give the room a warm and intimate feel.

On the floor, parquet is an almost natural choice. Depending on its color, light or dark, you will choose a rug of either a warm or pale color, and of course one that is in harmony with the walls. If you are a fan of *wabi-sabi*, consider terracotta tiles, which are certainly less warm to the touch than parquet, but have the advantage of keeping rooms cool in the summer. Even when industrially produced, floor tiles never look uniform and thus always provide a nice degree of visual interest.

The lighting system must be flexible enough to match any kind of atmosphere you want to create. You may favor a muted and relaxing light in the morning, or, on the contrary, you may enjoy a dazzlingly bright room to start the day. Plan for several lamps (and not just a central ceiling light): bedside lamps, a floor lamp (or several) equipped with a dimmer switch, and possibly a wall lamp in a corner dedicated to reading.

When choosing furniture, the equation to be solved is the right balance between pragmatism and comfort, simplicity and warmth, order and singularity. Our bedroom is the room in the house where we spend the most time, even if it is just to sleep. It is therefore essential that it be furnished according to our needs and desires. Indulge yourself, get rid of the superfluous, but with a certain leniency for the objects you value.

Above all, try to create a sense of space, both horizontally and vertically, avoiding, for example, cabinets and wardrobes that are too tall and therefore dominate the room. A Japanese bed, low enough and reduced to an elegant frame with a mattress on top, is the archetype of simple, functional furniture. If you want to limit the furnishings to the essentials, the list is quite succinct: bedside tables, an armchair, a chest of drawers. A nice set in the mid-century style will do perfectly. If you have a large room, a coffee table, a mirror, a stool, and houseplants will complete the decoration.

Above: Harmonious, soft colors provide a restful atmosphere.

Page 127: Intimate and warm, this very simple bedroom is nonetheless full of charm thanks to the bright colors that predominate and the presence of an original ceiling light.

Opposite: The simplicity of this bedroom is softened by a lighting system that transforms the ceiling into a cloudy sky.

GROWING UP IN A COZY ATMOSPHERE

In Japan, as in the Nordic countries, it is common practice for parents to spend a lot of time with their children. Family games and educational activities are central to the development of a child's personality. Social and group learning is another fundamental point that brings the two cultures together: in Japan, the emphasis is placed on respect for others and the importance of discipline, while Scandinavian education tends to give children responsibility and encourage initiative.

The space in which children evolve plays a key role in discovery of the world and its perception by the little ones. They will therefore benefit from a calm environment, with light and cheerful colors, where the objects are adapted to their needs and capacities, without superfluous elements that create unnecessary obstacles. One of the essential tasks specific to the design of a child's room is, of course, to organize a good storage system that can be used by the youngsters themselves.

The principles of Japandi style – simplicity, functionality, harmony, soft colors, and sustainable natural materials – seem tailor-made for a child's room. Everything should be done to stimulate the senses and create a joyful and serene atmosphere. Light-colored wood and materials that are pleasant to the touch, including textiles, as well as rounded, smooth shapes, create a space that is safe for young children. The furniture should be scaled to the size of the children whenever possible to free up the walls and provide a sense of space.

A soft light should bathe the room, but make sure it is of sufficient intensity. Finally, the atmosphere of a child's room should be as playful as possible, with a play mat and cushions for moments of rest.

Pages 130-31: Young children's bedrooms are a space for play and discovery, but also the refuge for their dreams.

For a teenager's bedroom, the emphasis will be on durable, evolving, and functional furniture. Space is an essential element because the room is the "territory" of the young person.

For teenagers, the Japandi spirit has at least two advantages that will encourage them to revisit the decoration of their room: first, the emphasis is placed on durable furniture and objects made of sustainable materials, a theme in line with the concerns of the younger generation about our planet; secondly, the sense of comfort combined with functionality, two characteristics of the style, are the guarantors of a well-being that is essential for their development. The design should revolve around three poles: a bed, a desk, and a relaxation area.

A low bed, with a wooden base or on a stand, will familiarize teenagers with the notion of minimalism. The desk should be the touch of originality that befits a teenager's room: why not choose a trestle table, elegant but very simple, accompanied by an ergonomic wooden chair with generous armrests? The set will be completed by a beautiful table lamp and shelves. The relaxation area can easily be limited to a very comfortable armchair for reading, listening to music, or simply daydreaming. Add a rug to give a little warmth to the floor. In terms of storage, a closet built into a wall is ideal so as not to encroach on the teenager's territory, but wooden or Plexiglas chests, which can be adjusted, offer another good practical solution.

THE KITCHEN: FUNCTIONALITY FIRST AND FOREMOST

Looking at images of Japanese or Nordic kitchens, one is often surprised by their dazzling cleanliness and spacious, orderly character. The image that emerges is that of a laboratory rather than a place where people cook and share meals. However, beyond the minimalist simplicity that unites the design of kitchens in Japan and Scandinavia, it is the functional aspect that prevails in both cases.

White is the dominant color in a Nordic kitchen. It has the advantage of offering some useful extra brightness and of leaving no chance for small stains or dirt. The furniture, if not white, is made of light wood, for the same reasons. Small pops of color – lamps, for example – may be used to enliven the room. In Japan, wood is the first choice when it comes to the decoration of the kitchen: from the cupboards to the worktop, pine, or any other light wood, sets the tone. The walls are painted in neutral colors – beige or light gray, for example. To save space, some shelves are suspended from the ceiling, especially above the worktop if it forms a central island. The goal is to eliminate anything that would overload the surfaces where food is prepared, including utensils and small appliances.

Lighting plays a key role, as it is always helpful to have direct light for food preparation. If your kitchen is small, or if the windows are not very wide, consider installing mirror tiles or a large adhesive mirror on one of the walls for a significant addition of light and the illusion of more space.

The tableware, even if it is not strictly part of the furnishings, should ideally follow the Japandi spirit. Feel free to select plates, glasses, cups, and cutlery with clean shapes, but make sure they are very functional. They can be chosen in light colors other than white to highlight the dishes. It goes without saying that wooden utensils are practically a must. If you want to add a little touch of *hygge* comfort, there's nothing to stop you from replacing some of the chairs around the kitchen table with light benches complemented by monochrome cushions.

The kitchen is a central room in any home, a place full of life and activity. Above all, it must be functional and perfectly lit.

To give an original touch to a kitchen, think of green plants and lighting that is out of the ordinary.

A BATHROOM FOR BODY AND MIND

In Japan, bathing is a true ritual designed not only to cleanse the body but also to rid oneself of the worries and stress of the day. Relaxation is actually the more important part of the ritual: after cleansing oneself with soap under a shower and rinsing off, one plunges into the bathtub intended for soaking, to rest and regenerate the body and mind. Some people compare the bathing custom to a meditation session in which one gradually detaches oneself from everyday problems to reconnect with one's inner self. A bathroom in the Japandi spirit should therefore include a shower area for washing, and a bath – in either wood or ceramic – for relaxation.

As in any bathroom, the possibility of moving around unhindered is essential: you should be able walk without bumping into decorative elements, while at the same time it is key to give the room a peaceful atmosphere that encourages relaxation.

Above: Despite the division between the shower area and the rest of the bathroom, the space is designed for seamless movement from one area to the other.

Opposite: Everything in a bathroom should be designed to facilitate the movement of those who use it. Properly installed, mirrors can help make the room look larger.

Overleaf: This Japandi-style bathroom by French brand Grandbains is a perfect example of a relaxing space, with its light partitions, storage shelves built into the walls, and a bathtub to rest in after a long day.

Pages 142–43: Choose lightweight storage pieces made of wood, bamboo, or wicker.

A reasonably minimalist approach is the best way to achieve this, and the ideal is to limit the bathroom design to five elements: a shower, soaking tub, sink, discreet storage space, and a stool for changing clothes.

Depending on the material used for the floor, you can add a mat for extra comfort and warmth. For the walls and floor, the choice of materials should be based on two imperatives: ease of maintenance to ensure that the bathroom is always clean, and a warm and intimate appearance. If you opt for wooden panels, make sure that they are varnished and treated against moisture. For the floor, nonslip tiles are a safe bet. Give priority to natural light, with opaque glass, for example, and add some indirect, adjustable lighting. The storage unit can consist of shelves around the sink, with a closable wicker basket for clean towels. You can also consider a low cabinet made of bamboo or a wall-mounted cupboard with inconspicuous doors.

The dominant color should be light, but not necessarily a shade of white: you can try pale gray or blue. Consider adding darker touches to create contrast and give the room some warmth and originality. A green plant will give the bathroom a lively and natural look, and you will be able to admire its beauty while bathing.

A COMFORTABLE HOME OFFICE

Unless you have a whole room at your disposal, you'll need a little skill to set up a home office in a living room, hallway, or bedroom without letting the workspace affect the atmosphere of the place. A desk, an ergonomic chair, a computer monitor, and especially a printer or cables do not easily go unnoticed in a house. The sight of a computer mouse or a pile of files is not likely to create a feeling of peace and quiet; a poorly set-up home office can spoil the atmosphere of a room. However, no one would genuinely prefer to work from a garage workbench, in a converted broom closet, or in the attic, because your home workplace should have adequate lighting, a reasonable amount of space, and an environment that facilitates concentration and creativity. You also need to be able to adopt a good posture that will prevent you from the pain of prolonged sitting.

Just think about the principles of Japandi style and you will understand that the solution to this complex equation follows quite logically: simplicity, functionality, and comfort are all elements to be taken into account to create a pleasant home office that is as understated in its look as possible.

A desk with very simple lines and a few decorative objects can be used to create a discreet home office. The secretary, a piece of furniture with a folding desk, is an excellent choice since it offers a workspace when open, and storage space when closed.

One of the most suitable pieces of furniture for this purpose is the classic secretary desk, which, when open, offers a reasonably sized table for work. When closed, it will keep your files and equipment out of sight. If you like to stretch out your legs under your desk, opt for a model with legs, which is lighter. Models with drawers under the desk are a little less comfortable, but provide plenty of storage space, especially for a printer or some office equipment. There are secretary desks of all sizes and in sufficiently varied styles that one of them will fit in the room in which it is to be installed, even if its look does not necessarily match pure Japandi norms. If you have very little room space, but have closets or a large storage area, you may want to consider a folding table with a light and simple structure. The advantage of this choice is that you can keep a certain freedom of movement: as soon as the nice weather arrives, or according to your activities, your office corner can be moved without hindrance to a terrace or to any other room of the house. The only drawback is that you'll have to put it away after each working session.

A well-designed folding table takes up as little space as a clothes-drying rack or an ironing board, for example. Another advantage of the folding table is that it is multifunctional and can serve as a side table on days when you have a large number of guests.

For the seat in your office, the ideal would be to find a model with a single central swivel leg and armrests, such as the iconic *Tulip* chair designed by Eero Saarinen in 1957 and still produced by Knoll. Failing that, any elegant chair, preferably wooden, with arms and a comfortable back will do.

A small wicker or cardboard storage box with a lid and two incised side openings will hide a power strip and the cables connected to it. Last but not least, a pretty floor lamp and some well-placed houseplants will give your home office a less austere look.

A TERRACE IN JAPANDI FASHION

Whether you have a terrace, a veranda, or a balcony, you can create a small green space in the Japandi spirit. Without going so far as to replicate a classic Japanese garden, it is quite easy to assemble wooden slabs and panels (or walls made of *shoji*, the translucent paper that is very common in Japanese interiors), pebbles, plants, and even a small pond that will form a place where you can recharge your batteries and spend some time communicating with nature. A bamboo hedge planted as a "screen" on the edge of a terrace or along a veranda wall will offer as many aesthetic advantages as practical ones: the foliage resists colder weather well, it keeps its light-green color during the gray months, and you will enjoy the delicate rustling of the stems and leaves in the wind. Dwarf or slow-growing plants offer the possibility of gathering a wide variety of botanical species in a limited space. You can choose from cacti, succulents such as aloe vera, aromatic plants (thyme, rosemary, lavender), and dwarf fruit trees.

Creating a pebble walkway may not seem obvious on a balcony or in a winter garden, but in addition to the pleasant contrast that the pebbles' rounded shapes and pale-gray color will offer with the wooden slabs, you will quickly appreciate the arch massages that tone up the blood circulation – if you walk barefoot or in socks, that is. A small pool can host water lilies or lotus flowers; despite its delicate appearance, the lotus plant is particularly hardy and resists cold winters well.

For outdoor furniture, wood will always be a natural option. You will have the choice between light woods, such as rattan, bamboo, and wicker with bright colors, and teak or other tropical species, which are darker and thicker but perfectly resistant to adverse weather. If you have very little space, opt for a canvas deckchair rather than a bench, with a folding table.

Above: Consider installing an outdoor sofa for enjoying nature.

Page 148: Cacti and succulents have the advantage of not taking up too much space and are easy to care for.

Page 149: A small garden area with a bamboo fence, decking, and a pebble walkway can be created in a compact space.

Opposite: A small terrace can be decorated with green plants in clay pots or wooden crates.

ACKNOWLEDGMENTS

This book gave us the opportunity to have inspiring meetings. We would like to express our gratitude to all the designers, artisans, creators, manufacturers, and managers of design brands who enthusiastically welcomed this project and offered us their unfailing support. They are too numerous to be mentioned individually here, but we thank them collectively from the bottom of our hearts.

Our gratitude also goes to the team at Éditions de La Martinière, the original French publisher, and to Hugh Merrell, who believed without hesitation in the success of an English edition. Thanks also to Allison S. Adelman for her accurate copy-editing and wise guidance.

NOTES

1. Quoted in Naomi Pollock, *Japanese Design since 1945: A Complete Sourcebook*, Thames & Hudson, 2020.
2. Okakura Kakuzō, *The Book of Tea*, 1906.
3. Leonard Koren, *Wabi-Sabi for Artists, Designers, Poets & Philosophers*, Imperfect Publishing, 2008.
4. Ibid.
5. Interview with French newspaper *Libération*, August 25, 2001.
6. Quoted in Sachiko Matsuyama, "*Shokunin* and Devotion," *Kyoto Journal*, September 22, 2018.

JAPANDI ON INSTAGRAM

@japandi_design
@japandihouse
@japandi.interior
@japandi_interior
@japandi.lights
@japandi.living
@japandistyle
@japandi.your.home

INSTAGRAM ACCOUNTS OF DESIGNERS AND MANUFACTURERS FEATURED IN THIS BOOK

1616/Arita: @1616_arita_japan
Akiko Ken Made: @akiko_ken_made
Anderssen & Voll: @anderssenvoll
Ariake: @ariake_collection
Asahiyaki: @asahiyaki
Cecilie Manz: @ceciliemanz
Claesson Koivisto Rune: @claessonkoivistorune
EO: @eo.dk
Fritz Hansen: @fritzhansen
Hiromichi Konno: @hiromichi_konno
Karimoku: @karimoku_official, @karimokucasestudy
Keiji Ashizawa: @keijiashizawadesign
Kojima: @kojima_shoten
Lars Vejen: @larsvejen
Motarasu: @_motarasu
Naoto Fukasawa: @naoto_fukasawa_design_ltd
nendo: @nendo_official
Norm Architects: @normarchitects
OEO Studio: @oeo_studio
Offecct: @offectofficial
Shuji Nakagawa: @shuji_nakagawa
Stilleben: @stilleben_dk
studioA27: @studioA27
Studio Kaksikko: @studio_kasikko
Taijiro Ishiko: @taijiro_ishiko
Teruhiro Yanagihara: @teruhiroyanagihara
Tsukasa Goto: @tsukasagoto

INDEX OF DESIGN OBJECTS

PHOTO CREDITS

p. 2: © runna10/iStock by Getty Images

p. 4: © Ellos, ellos.se

p. 7: © HAY, Klaus Langelund for HAY (photographer)

p. 8: © rawpixel

p. 11: © Katarzyna Bialasiewicz/iStock by Getty Images

p. 12: © rawpixel

pp. 14-15: © vicnt/iStock by Getty Images

p. 16: © Evelyn Müller

p. 18: © Katarzyna Bialasiewicz/iStock by Getty Images

p. 19: © rawpixel

pp. 20-21: © Navamin Keawmorakot/iStock by Getty Images

p. 22: © Kari Shea/Unsplash

p. 23: © ume ilus/iStock by Getty Images

p. 24: © Oriento/Unsplash

p. 25: © Eva Elijas/Pexels

p. 26: © Katarzyna Bialasiewicz/iStock by Getty Images

p. 27: © ACHITECTMADE

pp. 28-29, 31, 32-33, 35: © Katarzyna Bialasiewicz/iStock by
     Getty Images

p. 36 top: © Iittala

p. 36 bottom: © ARCHITECTMADE

p. 37: © Vitra

p. 39: © PP Møbler, Katja Kejser Pedersen & Kasper Holst

p. 40: © Rachel Claire/Pexels

p. 42: © Fritz Hansen

p. 44: © Ditte Isager, courtesy of OEO Studio

pp. 46-47, 48: © OEO Studio

p. 50: © Daisuke Yoshinari, courtesy of Oki Sato

p. 51: © Fritz Hansen

p. 52: © Inger Marie Grini, courtesy of Anderssen & Voll

pp. 53, 54, 55: © Ariake

p. 56: © Maya Matsuura, courtesy of Akiko Ken Made

pp. 58, 59, 60, 61: © Ole Akhøj, courtesy of Akiko Ken Made

p. 62: © Dejan Alankhan, courtesy of studioA27

pp. 63, 64, 65: © studioA27

p. 66: © Dejan Alankhan, courtesy of Design Studio
     Lars Vejen

pp. 67, 68, 69: © Design Studio Lars Vejen

p. 70: © Hiromichi Konno

pp. 71, 72, 73: © Softline

p. 74: © Knut Koivisto, courtesy of Claesson Koivisto Rune

pp. 75, 76, 77, 78, 79, 81: © Claesson Koivisto Rune

p. 82: © Naoto Fukasawa

p. 83: © HAY, Klaus Langelund for HAY (photographer)

p. 84: © Casper Sejersen, courtesy of Cecilie Manz

p. 85: © Elizabeth Heltoft Arnby/1616 Arita Japan, courtesy
     of Cecilie Manz

pp. 86-87: © CECILIE MANZ STUDIO

p. 88: © Offecct

p. 89: © Anneke Hymmen, courtesy of Teruhiro Yanagihara

pp. 90-91: © Offecct

p. 92: © Stilleben. Photograph by Magnus Ekstrøm

p. 93: © Motarasu

p. 94: © Alberto Strada, courtesy of Tsukasa Goto

p. 95: © Alberto Strada, courtesy of EO

p. 96: Mickael Vis, courtesy of Design Studio Kaksikko

p. 97: Chikako Harada, courtesy of Design Studio Kaksikko

p. 98: © Norm Architects

pp. 99, 100, 101: © Karimoku Case Study

pp. 102, 103: © Norm Architects

p. 104: © Steen Evald, courtesy of Mikkel Zebitz

pp. 106-107: © Motarasu. Location: Izumi, Frederiksberg

p. 108: © Maria Marinina

p. 111: © NelleG/iStock by Getty Images

p. 113: © Onurdongel/iStock by Getty Images

pp. 114-15: © Michinori Aoki, courtesy of OEO Studio

p. 116: © monkeybusinessimages/iStock by Getty Images

pp. 118, 119: © CreativaStudio/iStock by Getty Images

pp. 120-21: © Michinori Aoki, courtesy of OEO Studio

p. 122: © NelleG/iStock by Getty Images

p. 124: © Vanit Janthra/iStock by Getty Images

p. 125: © Follow The Flow/iStock by Getty Images

pp. 127, 128: © Katarzyna Bialasiewicz/iStock by Getty
     Images

First published in English in 2022 by
Merrell Publishers, London and New York

Merrell Publishers Limited
70 Cowcross Street
London EC1M 6EJ

merrellpublishers.com

First published as *L'Esprit Japandi: À la croisée des designs japonais et scandinave* in 2022 by Éditions de La Martinière, Paris

A catalogue record for this book is available from the Library of Congress.

British Library Cataloguing in Publication Data.
A catalogue record for this book is available from the British Library.

ISBN 978-1-8589-4706-8

Produced by Merrell Publishers Limited
Copy-edited by Allison Silver Adelman

Printed and bound in China

AGATA TOROMANOFF is an art and design historian who has curated numerous contemporary art projects. She is the author of several books, including *Chairs by Architects* (2016), *Sofas: 340 Iconic Designs* (2018), *Vases: 250 State-of-the-Art Designs* (2019), and *Designs for Children* (Merrell, 2022).

PIERRE TOROMANOFF studied mathematics and Russian literature. In 2014, after a career of more than twenty years in book publishing as international sales manager and then managing director of several art publishers, he cofounded a book-packaging agency with his wife, Agata. Since then, he has authored publications on art, design, architecture, and photography.